COWBOY
WISDOM

COWBOY WISDOM

**PROVERBS, ADVICE, LORE, YARNS,
AND LIES FROM ROY, GENE, AND
OTHER RIDERS OF THE HAPPY TRAIL**

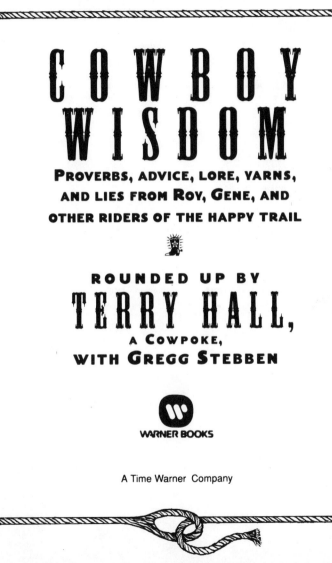

**ROUNDED UP BY
TERRY HALL,
A COWPOKE,
WITH GREGG STEBBEN**

WARNER BOOKS

A Time Warner Company

Copyright © 1995 by Modern Man Books
All rights reserved.

 A Time Warner Company

Warner Books, Inc., 1271 Avenue of the Americas, New York, NY 10020
Printed in the United States of America
First Printing: February 1995
10 9 8 7 6 5 4 3 2 1

Library of Congress Cataloging-in-Publication Data

Cowboy wisdom / rounded up by Terry Hall, with Gregg Stebben.
    p. cm.
  ISBN 0-446-67076-6
  1. Cowboys—United States—Quotations. I. Hall, Terry.
II. Stebben, Gregg.
F596.C8775 1995
818'.02—dc20   94-27254
                           CIP

Book design and decoration by L&G McRee
Cover design by Julia Kushnirsky
Cover illustration by Amelia Faulkner

To the lady who wears many hats.
TERRY HALL

To Ann Stebben—a true rodeo cowgirl.
GREGG STEBBEN

ACKNOWLEDGMENTS

We would like to thank the following people for their assistance: Claudia and Mike Riordan; Susan and Bill Streaker; Hal Cannon and Cyd McMullen of the Western Folklore Center of Elko, Nevada; C. J. Hadley and Benny Romero of *Range* magazine; Kathy Gangwisch; Kathy Lynn Wills of the Cowboy Country General Store; Charlotte Thompson; Jennifer Lyons; Judy Andreson; Rib, Pat, and Wylie Gustafson; Harry Rinker; Ted Hake of Hake's Americana & Collectibles; F. E. Abernathy of the Texas Folklore Society; and Heather Bach.

Grateful acknowledgment is given for permission to quote from the following:

Selections from *Great American Folklore* by Kemp P. Battle. Copyright ©1986 by Kemp Battle. Used with permission of Doubleday Book & Music Clubs, Inc. "The Coyote: Animal and Folk-Character," by Lillian Elizabeth Barclay from *Coyote Wisdom*, edited by J. Frank Dobie, Mody C. Boatwright, and Harry H. Ransom, Publications of the Texas Folklore Society Number 14, 1938; "Fifty Thousand Mustangs" by Frank Collinson (originally published in *Ranch Romances*, March and November 1936), "Mustanging on the Staked Plains, 1887" by Homer Hoyt (originally published in *The Colorado Magazine*, March 1934), "Black Kettle" by Frank M. Lockard (originally published by R. G. Wolfe, 1924), and "A Mustanger of 1850" by J. W. Moses (originally published in the *San Antonio Express*,

April 1888) from *Mustangs and Cow Horses*, edited by J. Frank Dobie, Mody C. Boatwright, and Harry H. Ransom, Publications of the Texas Folklore Society Number 16, 1940; "Ranch Remedios" by Frost Woodhull from *Man, Bird and Beast,* edited by J. Frank Dobie, Publications of the Texas Folklore Society Number 8, 1930. All reprinted by permission of the Texas Folklore Society.

Grateful acknowledgment is also given for use from the following: *A Son of the Frontier* by John Abernathy; *Calamity Jane and the Lady Wildcats* by Duncan Aikman; *Vanishing Breed* by William Albert Allard; *Captain George Ash* by George Ash; *Back in the Saddle Again* by Gene Autry; *The American West* by Lucius Beebe and Charles Clegg; *Cow by the Tail* by Jesse James Benton; *Riding the Mustang Trail* by Forrester Blake; *Cowboy Life on the Western Plains* by Edgar Beecher Bronson; *Wondrous Times on the Frontier* by Dee Brown; *An Old Time Cowboy* by London Brown; *Muggins, the Cow Horse* by Charles Camp; *Stunt Man* by Yakima Canutt; *Arizona Cowboys* by Dane Coolidge; *Old California Cowboys* by Dane Coolidge; *Range Rider* by Bud Cowan; *Cow Country* by Edward Everett Dale; *Cowboy Culture* by David Dary; *The Autobiography of Will Rogers* by Donald Day; *Cowboy Fun* by Frank Dean; *The Flavor of Texas* by J. Frank Dobie; *A Vaquero of the Brush Country* by J. Frank Dobie and John Young; *Cattle Kings of Texas* by C. L. Douglas; *Great Trails of the West* by Richard Dunlop; *A Corral Full of Stories* by Joe M. Evans; *Out West* by Mike Flanagan; *Once a Cowboy* by Walt Garrison and John Tullius; *The Cowboy Encyclopedia* by Bruce Grant; *An Overland Journey* by Horace

Greeley; *Box-Office Buckaroos* by Robert Heide and John Gilman; *The Bad Man of the West* by George D. Hendricks; *The Humor of the American Cowboy* by Stan Hoig; *They Went Thataway* by James Horwitz; *The Drifting Cowboy* by Will James; *Cowgirls: Women of the American West* by Teresa Jordan; *Rodeo: The Sport of the Cow Country* by Max Kegley; *The Official John Wayne Reference Book* by Charles John Kieskalt; *Long Lance* by Chief Buffalo Child Long Lance; *Cowboy Songs and Other Frontier Ballads* by J. A. and Alan Lomax; *Women of the West* by Cathy Luchetti and Carol Olwell; *The Life and Legend of Tom Mix* by Paul E. Mix; *The Book of the American West* by Jay Monaghan; *Honky Tonk Angel: The Intimate Story of Patsy Cline* by Ellis Nassour; *Fifty Years on the Trail* by John Young Nelson as described to Harrington O'Reilly; *Wild Bill Hickok* by Richard O'Connor; *The Outlaw Trail* by Robert Redford; *The Roll Away Saloon* by Roland W. Rider as told to Deirdre Murray Paulsen; *The Cowgirls* by Joyce Gibson Roach; *The Cowboy* by Philip Ashton Rollins; *The Book of Cowboys* by Francis Rolt-Wheeler; *The Open Range* and *Bunk House Philosophy* by Oscar Rush; *The Lives and Legends of Buffalo Bill* by Don Russell; *The Settlers' West* by Martin F. Schmitt and Dee Brown; *El Rodeo* by Charles Simpson; *The Kaw* by Floyd Streeter; *Clint Eastwood Riding High* by Douglas Thompson; *Cowboys of America* by Sanford Tousey; *Queen of Cowtowns* by Stanley Vestal; *The Cowboy at Work* by Fay E. Ward; and *Dodge City* by Robert M. Wright.

CONTENTS

NOTE

This is a little collection of this and that and other things a cowboy knows, but that other folks might not. The things in this book have been learned the hard way, and I hope they help. Sometimes, a fellow will get out alone on the trail and get too hot or too wet or too dry and just plain go stupid because there's not a smart cowboy around to make him see straight. That's why this book has been designed to fit in a standard-sized saddlebag. It's what you call your basic Cowpoke's Companion.

There's not much in here from guys who talk cowboy, but aren't, or from guys who dress cowboy, but aren't. Cowboys think people who act like cowboys but aren't are a pain in the behind, probably the same way proctologists can't stand being around guys who talk and dress like proctologists, but aren't.

To get in this book, you either have to be a cowboy, or you have to be somebody a cowboy would like to be.

There are also some things in here from women we call cowgirls, since that seems like the right way to call a person who does everything a cowboy does, but looks better doing it. Nowadays, these people are also called cow-women or cowpersons—but only by people who aren't cowboys or cowgirls. Nothing like a good bounce on a hard saddle to knock the political correctness right out of a person.

Anyway, if you've eaten enough dust to recognize where it came from by taste alone, you know who you are. Hope you and all your friends enjoy this little ride.

—TERRY HALL
Hastings, Nebraska

1
LIFE

A man's gotta do what a man's gotta do.
—ALAN LADD
Hollywood, California
in *Shane*
1953

GUIDANCE FROM A BUNCH OF BOYS NAMED ROGERS

• All you have in life is your word, your handshake, and the image you portray.

—DUSTY ROGERS

• Civilization has taught us to eat with a fork, but even now if nobody is around we use our fingers.

—WILL ROGERS

• Give 90 percent and take 10 percent on both sides. That's the way to get along with your horse or your wife.

—ROY ROGERS

COWBOY COLLEGE

I contend that a year spent on the hurricane deck of a cow pony is one of the most useful and valuable pieces of experience a young man can possibly have in fitting himself for business of almost any kind; and if I were educating a boy to fight the battle of his life, I would secure him a cowboy's situation as soon as he was through with his studies at school. A term of service on a frontier cattle ranch will take the conceit out of any boy; it will at the same time teach him self-reliance; it will teach him to endure hardships and suffering; it will give him nerve and pluck; it will develop the latent energy in him to a degree that could not be accomplished by any other apprenticeship or experience that I know of. Many of the most successful businessmen in the Western towns of today served their first years on the frontier as "cow punchers," and to that school they owe the firmness of character and the ability to surmount great obstacles that have made their success in life possible.

—*Tribune-Republican*
Denver, Colorado
1886

quoted by Clifford Westermeier in
Trailing the Cowboy

Son, if you're going to be a cowboy, let me give you two pieces of advice: Stick to herding steers—never work for a cow-and-calf outfit. And never work for a man who has electricity in his barn. You'll be up all night.

—Anonymous
quoted by William Albert Allard
in *Vanishing Breed*
1982

Every cowboy thinks he knows more than every other cowboy. But the only thing they all know for sure is when's payday and where's grub.

—L. L. Royster
Amarillo, Texas
1915

I worked around cattle all my life, and I guess I learned all there is to know about it, and I think I can sum it all up in one thing: You can't drink coffee on a running horse—and a good thing, too.

—SAMUEL BRENNER
Lubbock, Texas
1962

You raise kids, dogs, and horses all the same.

—RAY FARMER
Elko, Nevada
c. 1964

RULES OF THE RANGE

The Roy Rogers Riders Club Rules

1. Be neat and clean.
2. Be courteous and polite.
3. Always obey your parents.
4. Protect the weak and help them.
5. Be brave but never take chances.
6. Study hard and learn all you can.
7. Be kind to animals and care for them.
8. Eat all your food and never waste any.
9. Love God and go to Sunday School regularly.
10. Always respect our flag and our country.

—ROY

Gene Autry's Cowboy Code

1. The cowboy must never shoot first, hit a smaller man, or take unfair advantage.
2. He must never go back on his word, or a trust confided in him.
3. He must always tell the truth.
4. He must be gentle with children, elderly people, and animals.
5. He must not advocate or possess racially or religiously intolerant ideas.
6. He must help people in distress.
7. He must be a good worker.
8. He must keep himself clean in thought, speech, action, and personal habits. He must neither drink or smoke.
9. He must respect women, parents, and his nation's laws.
10. He must be a patriot.

—GENE

Hopalong Cassidy's Troopers' Creed for Boys and Girls

I promise:

- To be kind to birds and animals,
- To always be faithful and fair,
- To keep myself neat and clean,
- To always be courteous,
- To be careful when crossing streets,
- To avoid bad habits,
- To study and always learn my lessons,
- To obey my parents.

—HOPPY

HOUSE RULES

These are the rules and regulations of this hotel.

- This house will be considered strictly intemperate.
- Persons owing bills for board will be bored for bills.
- Boarders who do not wish to pay in advance are requested to pay in advance.
- Boarders are requested to wait on the colored cook for meals.
- Sheets will be nightly changed once in six months—oftener if necessary.
- Boarders are expected to pull off their boots if they can conveniently do so.
- Beds with or without bedbugs.

All moneys and other valuables are to be left in charge of the proprietor. This is insisted upon, as he will be held responsible for no losses.

—Posted at a
Dodge City, Kansas, hotel
c. 1888

Talk low, talk slow, and don't say too much.

—JOHN WAYNE

You know, once, a long time ago, my dad told me something that I never have forgot. He told me that if all I knowed was cows and horses, then I better not try to put something over on a feller if I have to get off the subject of cows and horses to do it.

—RILEY
Texas panhandle
1932

One day, I reviewed my life as a cowboy from every angle and came to the conclusion that all I had gained was experience, and I could not turn that into cash, so I decided I had enough of it, and made up my mind to go home, get married, and settle down to farming.

—F. M. POLK
Luling, Texas
c. 1925

My dearest Louisa—
Well I have found work as a cow-boy here and as soon as I
find honest work I will send for you and Sarah. . . .

—CHARLES SMITH
Bagdag Ranch, Texas
1891

The cowboy gets up early in the morning, decides what he
wants to do, then straddles his pony and gets to work. He does
the best he can and spends as little money as possible.

The politician gets up late in the morning, straddles the
fence, spends all the money he can, gets all the votes lined up,
and then decides what to do.

—JOE M. EVANS
El Paso, Texas
1939

I've always acted alone. Americans admire that enormously. Americans admire the cowboy leading the caravan alone, the cowboy entering a village alone on his horse.

—HENRY KISSINGER

It's easy to say there are no atheists in foxholes, but it's not as easy to say there are no atheists riding behind the back side of a herd.

—LUTHER ROBINSON
Tulsa, Oklahoma
1970

COWBOY DEATH

When life is over and my race is run,
When death shadows gather and my time has come,
When I've rode my last horse and have turned my last steer,
When my soul has winged its way to that celestial sphere,
When my grave has been dug and I've been laid to rest,
Please let it be in the far, far West.

—J. E. McCauley
Seymour, Texas
1924

I want no fenced-in graveyard
With snorin' souls about—
Just cache me in the desert
When my light goes out.

—Anonymous

Oh, beat the drum slowly
And play the fife lowly,
Play the dead march as you carry me along;
Take me to the green valley,
There lay the sod o'er me,
For I'm a young cowboy and know I've done wrong.

       —"The Cowboy's Lament"
       TRADITIONAL

They say there will be a great round-up,
And cowboys, like dogies, will stand,
To be mavericked by the Riders of Judgment
Who are posted and know every brand.

I know there's many a stray cowboy
Who'll be lost in at the great final sale,
When he might have gone in green pastures
had he known the dim narrow trail.

I wonder if ever a cowboy
Stood ready for that Judgment Day
And could say to the Boss of the Riders,
"I'm ready, come drive me away."

They say He will never forget you,
That He knows every action and look;
So, for safety, you'd better get branded,
Have your name in his big Tally Book,

To be shipped to that bright mystic region,
Over there in the green pastures to lie,
And be led by the crystal still waters
To the home in the sweet by-and-by.

The road to that far happy region
Is a dim narrow trail, so they say;
But the bright one that leads to perdition
Is posted and blazed all the way.

—TRADITIONAL

2

TRAIL LORE

THE UNIVERSAL
BOVINE TRAIL BOSS COMMAND:

Head 'em up! Move 'em out!

—ERIC FLEMING
as trail boss Gil Favor
on TV's *Rawhide*
1968

One thing I'll say fer the West is that in this country there is more cows and less butter, more rivers and less water, and you can look farther and see less than in any other place in the world.

—ANONYMOUS
Arizona rancher
c. 1900

ROWLAND RIDER'S TEN-POINT COWBOY CHECKLIST

To become a good cowboy in certain areas, there's ten rules that you've got to comply with before you get your silver spurs:

1. Handle a lariat correctly.

2. Rope an unbroken horse within the corral and break it to lead.

3. Saddle a horse correctly. Also, properly set and cinch a pack saddle. And after that, you have to know how to guide a horse with one hand and also to guide him with your knees.

4. Properly pack an animal, including throwing the diamond hitch. This means cinching, in the shape of a diamond, the ends of the rope that holds the pack saddle.

5. How to approach a horse or mule to hobble it: It isn't easy. You walk up to a horse with your head down and your hobbles in your hand. You don't look him in the eye. You just walk up and crouch and go down and put the hobbles on him and step back.

6. Memorize the local brands of the area and their position on the animal.

7. Know and be able to perform the proper procedure to rope and stretch out an animal for branding and marking.

8. How to use a "branding ring"—the proper temperature and method: The hotter the ring, the faster you can make the brand; it should be a good cherry red, and that's about as hot as you can get it in a brush fire.

9. Proper identification of cow and calf to insure proper ownership before branding. You let the mother cow search out the calf in the herd, and the calf will follow at her side.

10. To ride a cutting horse without "pulling leather" after the rider has indicated to the horse which animal is to be cut from the herd.

—ROWLAND RIDER
Arizona Strip
1909

AB BLOCKER'S COWBOY CATECHISM

- Can you ride a pitching bronc?
- Can you rope a horse out of the remuda without throwing the loop around your own head?
- Are you good-natured?
- In case of a stampede at night, would you drift along in front or circle the cattle to a mill?
- Can you sing?

—Trail boss AB BLOCKER's questions
put to a prospective rider
San Antonio, Texas
c. 1880

[To move a herd] the leader works in the open, and the boss in covert. The leader leads, and the boss drives.

—TEDDY ROOSEVELT
1898

The only comparison I can make between moving a bunch of cows across the range and moving a bill through Congress is that if you're behind a bunch of cows you can give them direction, but behind a piece of legislation, it's a free-for-all.

So I'm leaving politics. I'm getting the hell out of Washington and going back to my ranch in Oregon, where there's some stability and judgment left in the world.

—CONGRESSMAN ROBERT SMITH
Washington, D.C.
1994

In the summer of 1869, I sold a bunch of grown steers in Palo Pinto County, Texas, to Dr. D. B. Warren of Missouri, and we trailed them to Baxter Springs, Kansas. We swam Red River at the old Preston ferry. We camped near the river the night before and tried to cross early in the morning. The river was very full of muddy water, and the cattle refused to take to the water. After all hands had about exhausted themselves, Dr. Warren, who was his own [trail] boss, said to me, "William, what will we do about it?" I answered him that we had better back out and graze the cattle until the sun got up so they could see the other bank, and they would want water and go across. "You should know that you can't swim cattle across as big a stream as this going east in the morning or going west late of an evening with the sun in their faces." About one P.M. we put them back on the trail and by the time the drags got near the river, the leaders were climbing the east bank. The doctor looked at me and said, "Well, I'll be damned. Every man to his profession."

—W. E. CURETON
Meridian, Texas
1891

[On the Chisholm Trail] it kept raining and storming. Good horses were ruined for life. All the horses were ridden down. There was no such thing as lying down in a dry bed for a few hours of unbroken sleep. The cow chips, our principal fuel, were all wet and half the time we could not get enough hot food and coffee. In such times a cowboy swore that he'd never go up the trail again....

So, if when he got to town, after long months out in the brush, on the lone prairie, or on the long, long trail, the cowboy "cut loose" and had "a little fun," he can hardly be blamed.

—JOHN YOUNG
Alpine, Texas
1929

I never forgot that no matter how wet I was, no matter how sick I got, or how long I went between baths and shaves, no matter how much my horse said I stunk, I always remembered that, thank God, I still had my good looks.

—CALE WILKINS
Winslow, Arizona
1975

Keep your end up or turn in your string of horses. On the roundup, no soldiering goes; sick or well, it's hit yourself in the flank with your hat and keep up with the bunch or be set afoot to pack your saddle; there's no room in the chuck wagon for a quitter's blankets, and no time to close herd sick ones. So for heaven's sake don't start out unless you have the guts to stand it.

—N. R. DAVIS
Cheyenne, Wyoming
c. 1870

I have been on cow hunts when there were as many as one hundred men working together from different counties. Stockmen of today do not know anything about the hard work and strenuous times we encountered in those days. Sometimes we would be out for weeks at a time, starting every morning at daylight, and probably not getting in before dark, tired and hungry, and having to do without dinner all day. Our fare consisted of cornbread, black coffee, and plenty of good beef.

—WILLIAM J. BENNETT
Pearsall, Texas
1920

Of all places in the world, traviling in the mountains is the most apt to breed contentions and quarrils. The only way to keep out of it is to say but little, and mind your own business exclusively.

—ANONYMOUS
Colorado
c. 1870

All range is not the same, nutrients and conditions vary greatly; and all country is not of equal value. Where a cowboy in eastern Montana may be able to run a cow per acre, it might take twenty acres to run a cow in Western Colorado, and fifty acres more to run a single bovine in the deserts of the Great Basin.

—C. J. HADLEY
Publisher-Editor, *Range* Magazine
Carson City, Nevada
1994

A typical cowboy direction: "Head out to that juniper, turn left, go west to the Rocky Mountains and may the Good Lord bless your skies."

—ROBERT REDFORD
Hole-in-the-Wall, Wyoming
1975

You get yourself lost and you're playing with trouble. No matter whether you're out on a high plain or down in some forest, you got to find water to find your way home. What I do is I scout out a trail broke by any grazing animal—don't matter whether it's deer or cattle or what—and follow that trail, because it eventually leads to water. Then, when you find a little stream or creek or whatever it is, you follow it down a valley, and not up. Going up a valley takes you nowhere but nearer to God, and that's what you want to avoid, frankly. But if you follow water downstream far enough, you'll come to people, guaranteed. Of course, they may be lost, too. In fact, most people are lost most of the time, so if you're one of 'em, don't feel too bad.

—F. M. MEAGHER
Virginia City, Montana
1921

[Before bedding down for the night] find out what relief you are to go on, who to call and where they will sleep, so you won't be waking up everybody in camp to find the right man. It makes a cowpuncher fighting mad to wake him up from his needed sleep when not wanted.

Sleep with pants on and stuffed in your socks. Never take the spurs off your boots. Put your boots down first, your chaps on top of them, and your jacket over all for a pillow. It's nice to leave your boots outside in the weather and find when you try to pull them on in a hurry that they are either froze stiff as dry rawhide or full of rainwater.

Have everything ready to rise up, fling on, and skin out like a flash of lightening if there is a stampede, or to get out on time when you are called to go on guard. Remember that the safety of the herd depends on good ponies and good men ready to roll the instant they are needed. If the cattle are restless and there is liability of a stampede, you'd better go to bed just as you are—hat, jacket, pants, boots, spurs, chaps; and if snowing, or raining, your slicker, too—all on. A cowpuncher can sleep anyhow.

—*Trinidad Weekly News*
Trinidad, Colorado
July 20, 1882

You have to be careful how you wake a cowboy. Some men will kill you if you touch 'em while they're sleeping, kill you before they even open their eyes to see who's there. Most times, somebody'd just yell loud, and that was safer. My favorite jump-up holler was, "Wake up, snakes, and bite the biscuit!" That got me up right quick.

—LADDY NEWMAN
Aurora, Colorado
1911

To understand ranch lingo all yuh have to do is know in advance what the other feller means an' then pay no attention to what he says.

—PHILIP ASHTON ROLLINS
Cheyenne, Wyoming
1922

TRAIL REMEDIES

• **_Rheumatism:_** Take an empty whiskey bottle about half full of vinegar; put in a handful of large red ants. Shake well and apply internally and externally.

—MRS. GEO. R. GILLETTE
San Antonio, Texas
1890

• **_Whooping cough:_** Drink liberal quantities of mare's milk.

—MARVIN HUNTER
Bandera, Texas
c. 1900

• **_Foot rot in goats:_** Make a mixture of the following in an old wooden bucket: Two teaspoonfuls of alum, two and one-half teaspoonfuls of turpentine and one and a half gallons of water. Wash the goat's feet in this. It is enough for one hundred goats.

—ANONYMOUS PAMPHLET
c. 1890

• **Horse tetanus:** Founder and lockjaw caused by overheating can be cured by driving eighteen or twenty nails—make three rows of them—in a board so that the sharp points stick out from a quarter to half an inch. Then lay the board on the horse's forehead and hit the board with a hammer. I have seen my father cure more than a hundred horses which had lock-jaw by hitting this board a wallop.

—JOHN GRISSOM
San Antonio, Texas
1888

• **Blisters from hot grease, or for frostbitten feet, fingers, or ears:** Scrape a raw Irish potato and apply to the parts affected.

—ALBERT WEST
Uvalde, Texas
c. 1890

• **Toothache:** A chaw of tobacco's good.

—HOPALONG CASSIDY

• **Worse toothache:** Cut the first skin off the "frog" of a horse's front hoof, and then put the skin over the fire and char it until it crumbles, and put it in the tooth.

—PETE ANDERWALD
Bandera, Texas
c. 1900

• **Horse gas**: A positively O.K. remedy for colic in a horse is to take a tablespoon full of turpentine—or, if you'd rather, take two tablespoons full of turpentine—and put the turpentine in a shallow saucer, and then hold the saucer to the horse's navel. The astonishing thing about this remedio is the immediate disappearance of the turpentine. It disappears right while you're looking at it.

—FROST WOODHULL
San Antonio, Texas
c. 1930

• ***Baby colic:*** Take teaspoonful of soot in a cloth, pour over three tablespoonfuls of hot water, let steep a few minutes. Give baby teaspoonful every half hour.

—ANONYMOUS PAMPHLET
c. 1890

• ***Hair loss:*** One of the best hair tonics is to boil and wash the head with sotol (*Dasylirion texanum*). It will just make hair grow where there ain't no hair.

—FROST WOODHULL
San Antonio, Texas
c. 1930

• ***Hay Fever:*** An absolutely positive cure for hay fever is to smoke coffee grounds in a pipe.

—FROST WOODHULL
San Antonio, Texas
c. 1930

• *Pneumonia:* Take large cabbage leaves and wilt them over a fire to make them soft, then put the leaves all over the sick person's chest, sides, and back; wrap a thin cloth around them to hold the leaves on, then pour on vinegar just as hot as the patient can stand it. The patient will begin to sweat right away, and the pneumonia will be broken up.

—ANONYMOUS
quoted by Frost Woodhull

• *Chills:* Wear nutmeg on a string around the neck.

—ANONYMOUS PAMPHLET
c. 1890

• *Malaria:* The bark of the red-bud or Judas Tree may be used as a substitute for quinine.

—ELLEN SCHULZ
in *Texas Wild Flowers*

• **Skunk bite:** Cauterize the wound with hot iron. I know a Mexican who still lives here that was bitten on the hand while in camp alone one night. In telling us about it, he said that he tied a rope around his wrist and then...to a tree and burned the wound with a red-hot iron. Someone asked, "Why did you tie it to the tree?" And he said, "To keep me from running off."

—SHERIFF E. E. TOWNSEND
Brewster County
1901

• **Stammering:** To cure stammering, get child near an animal that is being butchered—hog, cow, anything—and as soon as the lights are cut out rub them vigorously in child's face, particularly about the mouth.

—FROST WOODHULL
San Antonio, Texas
c. 1930

• *Thirst:* A bullet in the mouth helps some, or a dime or quarter. Copper is the best, but the prickly pear is better than any of them; it keeps the mouth moist and agreeable longer than anything else we ever found.

And what to do with the rest of the prickly pear: If water is muddy and you wish to settle it, peel off stickers and [the] outside of the pear, slice, and scatter over the top of the water. They will soon sink to the bottom, carrying the sediment down with them.

—COLONEL CHARLES GOODNIGHT
Goodnight, Texas
1930

TRAIL MANNERS

I once heard Harry Halsell ask Roberts why he didn't stop cussing, and Jimmy explained that before he learned to cuss he had to shoot six or seven men who had cussed him.

—TOM YARBROUGH
Fort Worth, Texas
c. 1939

Cowboys had ethics and manners which were lived up to, under rules of the range. No cowboy was permitted to ask for food. The custom was to wait till the cook cried, "chuck-away!" Then there was a wild scramble and rattling of spurs as the cowboys rushed toward the end of the chuck wagon. The first cowboy to reach the wagon got the choice spaces between the spokes in the wagon wheel, in which to lay his six-shooter. None was permitted to eat without removing his guns.

No cowboy was permitted to use vile language or tell offensive stories while eating. Violation of this rule meant punishment, termed "putting the leggings on them," which consisted in placing the offender over the wagon-tongue and whipping him with leggings by the entire gang. If the cowboy resisted, his companions held his feet and hands while the lash was applied. Once punished in this manner, seldom did the cowboy ever violate the rule of the range a second time.

—JOHN "CATCH-'EM-ALIVE JACK" ABERNATHY
Austin, Texas
c. 1935

Know the rules in a cow camp when they have no regular cook. When anybody complains about the chuck they have to do the cooking. One cowboy broke a biscuit open and says, "They are burnt on the bottom and top and raw in the middle and salty as hell, but shore fine, just the way I like 'em."

—ANONYMOUS
Nebraska panhandle
c. 1880

CONTENTS OF A CHUCK WAGON

• ***In the wagon bed:*** Bedrolls, slickers, wagon sheet, 1/2-in. corral rope, guns, ammunition, lantern, kerosene, axle grease, extra wheel, salt pork, raw beef, green coffee beans, flour, pinto beans, sugar, salt, dried apples, onions, potatoes, grain for work team.

• ***In the tool box:*** Shovel, ax, branding irons, horseshoeing equipment, hobbles, rods for pot rack, extra skillets.

• ***In the chuck box and boot:*** Flour, sugar, dried fruit, roasted coffee beans, pinto beans, plates, cups, cutlery, castor oil, calomel, bandages, thread, needle, razor and strop, salt, lard, baking soda, vinegar, chewing tobacco, rolling tobacco, sourdough keg, matches, molasses, coffeepot, whiskey, skillets, Dutch ovens, pot hooks.

Some chuck wagons also had a small oven, and most had a water barrel.

—WILLIAM H. FORBIS
in *The Cowboys*
1973

DINNER

Sonofabitch Stew

2 pounds lean beef
Half a calf heart
1 1/2 pounds of calf liver
1 set sweetbreads
1 set brains
1 set marrow gut
Salt, pepper
Louisiana hot sauce

Kill off a young steer. Cut up beef, liver, and heart into 1-inch cubes; slice the marrow gut into small rings. Place in a Dutch oven or deep casserole. Cover meat with water and simmer for 2 to 3 hours. Add salt, pepper, and hot sauce to taste. Take sweetbreads and brains and cut in small pieces. Add to stew. Simmer another hour, never boiling.

Beans

- **2 pounds pinto beans**
- **2 pounds ham hock (or salt pork)**
- **2 onions, chopped**
- **4 tablespoons sugar**
- **2 green chilies (or to taste)**
- **1 can tomato paste**

Wash the beans and soak overnight. Drain, place in a Dutch oven, and cover with water. Add remaining ingredients and simmer until tender. Sample the beans while cooking. Add salt to taste and water as needed.

—adapted from *Cowpoke's Cookbook*
by ACE REID
Draggin's Ranch, Kerrville, Texas
1969

Prairie Oysters

Get everything off 'em, split 'em open, and fry 'em in hot fat
in a skillet until they are done good; then put salt on 'em and
serve 'em up hot.

—CHARLES WILLEY
Valentine, Nebraska
1877

Red Bean Pie

    1 cup cooked, mashed pinto beans
    1 cup sugar
    3 egg yolks, beaten
    1 cup milk
    1 teaspoon vanilla
    1 teaspoon nutmeg

Combine ingredients and place in uncooked pie crust. Bake at
350° for 30 minutes or until set. Make meringue with leftover
egg whites; spread on pie and brown in oven.

—adapted from *Cowpoke's Cookbook*
by ACE REID
Draggin' Ranch, Kerrville, Texas
1969

Sucamagrowl

This is a good substitute for pudding or pie.

- **3 cups of water**
- **2 cups of sugar**
- **2 pinches of cinnamon or nutmeg**
- **1 cup of vinegar**
- **2 tablespoons of flour**

First, put the water and vinegar together and bring to a boil. Mix the sugar and flour together and stir this mixture into the boiling liquid until it is thoroughly dissolved. Let cook for fifteen minutes and then add the spice. Have a dough ready, like a biscuit dough prepared with baking powder. Break it off by the tablespoonful and drop the pieces in the simmering liquid. When the dumplings are done serve them right off on tin plates while they're still hot.

—FAY WARD
Norfolk, Nebraska
1958

TRAIL GRACES

Eat yer meat and save the skin.
Turn up yer plates, and let's begin.
                              Amen.

Look out teeth! Look out gums!
Look out belly! Har she comes!
                              Amen.

That's the bread, that's the meat.
Now, by Joe, let's eat.
                              Amen.

COWBOY COFFEE

Take one pound of jamoka coffee and wet it good with water.
Boil it over a hot fire for thirty minutes, then pitch a horseshoe in. If the shoe sinks, put in more coffee.

—ANONYMOUS

A cowboy gets hungry enough, he'll go for his gun—and shoot fish.

—LAWRENCE CUBBIT
Laramie, Wyoming
1938

WHAT TO DO WITH A CATFISH AFTER YOU SHOOT IT

This is the kind of thing you learn in the music business that can come in handy in lots of different situations.

Cats are kind of slick when you get them out of the water and they have skin instead of scales like most fish, and you can work yourself to death on a five-pound catfish just trying to hold on to him and skin him at the same time. They also have sharp little barbs beneath their gills. So you want to get the cat under control so you can work with it.

1. Find a stump. The best way to skin a catfish is to find a stump and drive a nail through his head and into the stump. That'll stop the wiggling. Once you put the nail in his head, you pretty much took care of the old boy.

2. Use your knife to cut around his neck. You really want a good, sharp cut, so the skin comes off easy. But don't cut his head clear off, because if you cut his head off now, you've lost the use of your nail.

3. Take your pliers and start skinning. Now you see why you have to nail him to a stump. Otherwise, you can't hardly hold him. Trying to keep hold of a catfish while you work is a miserable way to try to skin one. You're trying to pull his skin off and he's falling on the ground all the time. You really need a stump and a nail.

4. Gut him. Turn him over onto his belly. I usually start cutting him from the bottom and work my way toward his head, but you can do it either way. You just put your knife in there and rip the belly up as you go along. It's kind of like cutting a piece of cloth—once you get started, it just goes on up. Then reach your fingers in there and gut him—everything comes out. It's almost like it was meant to be that way; there's very little attachment there. My gutting rule of thumb is, if it looks like something you don't want to eat, take it out.

Once you do that, *then* you cut the head off. Now, you've got a good, clean catfish.

—CHARLIE DANIELS
Lebanon, Tennessee
1993

FAMOUS COWBOY FOOD

Product	**Endorsed by**
• *Quaker Oats*	Roy Rogers
• *Peter Pan Peanut Butter*	Sky King
• *Langendorf Bread*	Red Ryder
• *General Mills Cereals*	Hopalong Cassidy
• *Grape Nuts*	Buck Jones
• *Wrigley chewing gum*	Wild Bill Hickok
• *Ralston Wheat Cereal*	Tom Mix

—WILLIAM SAVAGE
in *The Cowboy Hero*
1979

THE COMPLETE TRAIL KIT

I've got a good saddle blanket an' I used it fo' a bed all the way up heah, an' besides, if the weather's nice, that's bed enough, an' if it's stormin', any damn' fool knows he ought to be out with the cattle, an' cou'se he wants his slicker.

—JOHNNIE RIX
near Big Creek, Wyoming
c. 1887

For your horse, you need:

- A saddle
- A blanket
- A bridle
- A rope
- A bit
- A hackamore, and
- A smaller bosal.

For you, you'll need:

• A set of ropes for different purposes—for catching and branding calves, for roping bigger stock, all that kind of stuff.

• A good bed roll. Now, a bed roll serves two functions. First, it's where you do your sleeping. Second, it also acts as your suitcase. See, you just roll up your clothes inside of it, and tie it all up with a couple of straps or pieces of rope. Now, the bedroll itself is made out of a big piece of canvas. It's longer than it is wide. Find yourself a little mattress, like one of those army-type mattresses, and you wrap the mattress up in the canvas.

• Blankets and some old flannel sheets.

They did it the same way a hundred years ago—only the mattress was an old bag stuffed with straw that they had to change from time to time.

When you roll up your bedroll in the morning, it may be a good two feet around in diameter with all your clothes and everything in there—well, you can't take this big bedroll with you on your horse, so you put it on the chuck wagon until you need it again at the end of the day.

One other thing:

• A "possibles" bag, in which you've got everything for whatever might possibly happen: reloading equipment for your gun, a knife, and a bit of grub that'll keep you a few days if you ever need it.

—MIKE GERBER
Elko, Nevada
1994

Every cowboy carries a rope [and] when he is not using it, he keeps it tied to the right-hand side of the pommel of his saddle. In some places this rope is called a lasso. The spaniards called it *la reata*, which the cowboys shortened to "lariat." [It] may be made of hemp or maguey, or of four strands of rawhide wound together; it is often sixty feet long. The rawhide lariat must be handled with care; for, if a horse steps on it and breaks one of the strands, the lariat is weakened.

To lasso an animal the cowboy holds most of the rope in his left hand while he whirls the looped end at the animal. Then he takes a "dally," or twist around his saddlehorn, to hold the roped animal. With a short rope he does not take dallies, but keeps one end tied to the saddlehorn.

—SANFORD TOUSEY
New York City
1937

The ordinary length of a lasso is forty feet, though I frequently use one seventy-two feet in length. It is also fine exercise, the spinning of the rope bringing almost every muscle of the body into play. That it is light and can easily be carried, and the many things you can do with it make it an ideal article for all kinds of sports.

—CAPTAIN GEORGE ASH
London, England
1923

Every male person should have at least one rifle gun.

—ANONYMOUS
Advice from an emigrant guidebook
c. 1870

One good, sharp knife is worth two of almost anything else, except women and horses, of course.

—CHARLES JIMBY
XIT Ranch, Texas
c. 1885

HOW A COWPOKE KEEPS HIS EDGE

I can't remember ever learning how to sharpen a knife, myself—people were just always around filing or grinding their butcher knives all the time because they needed them sharp to slaughter the hogs and stuff. So learning how to sharpen a knife for me was sort of like learning to walk—everybody did it so I did it too, but I certainly don't remember taking my first step.

1. *Take an Arkansas hard-stone*—I guess they come from Arkansas—and put a spot of oil on it to keep the temper in the knife, to keep the friction from damaging the blade. Some guys use spit, but I use oil. The oil I use is called honing oil and it's made for that purpose. I've got a set of three stones, each

mounted in wood. One is a hard Arkansas, then there's a soft Arkansas, and then there's what they call a Washita, and it's just an extra little stone that you use. They're each about 4" x 16".

2. Take the stone and lay it down flat. Turn the blade of the knife toward you and bring the knife across the stone in a kind of circular motion, about a half moon. Then reverse it to sharpen the other side. You can tell whether you're getting an edge or not.

3. The angle is the most important part of the sharpening, and that's the thing that you just have to feel and learn. If you over-do it and hold the blade at too sharp an angle, you'll make the blade flat and you won't be sharpening anything—you'll just be wearing the blade out. If you don't have enough of an angle, you'll just make the knife duller. Get the angle right.

—CHARLIE DANIELS
Lebanon, Tennessee
1993

HOW TO EXTINGUISH A RANGE FIRE

One afternoon a puncher at Charles Goodnight's ranch in the Texas panhandle saw smoke boiling up to the south and raced toward it. When he arrived at the scene he found a gang of men beating at flames with wet gunny sacks, slickers, and brooms. When the fire refused to go out he and the other men attacked the blaze by a grisly but effective method: they shot a big steer, skinned him on one side and tied ropes to two legs. Then a pair of riders on either side of the fire line dragged the bloody carcass over it to quench the flames, like moving an eraser across a blackboard. The horses had to change sides frequently, or the one trotting on the burned patch might have been crippled by the charring of his hoofs.

—WILLIAM H. FORBIS
Bozeman, Montana
1973

COYOTE CAUTION

Indians say that coyote, unlike man, never kills wantonly, but only for food. As a matter of fact, given a chance, he may in an hour kill more kids out of a flock of goats than he can eat in a week. His business in life is not essentially different from that of man; namely, to find and get his daily meat.

—LILLIAN ELIZABETH BARCLAY
Waco, Texas
c. 1938

One man in a million can become a ventriloquist; every coyote is one at birth. He can so "place" his voice that you shall not know if it came from north, east, south, or west. As a multiplier—well, hearing one coyote, no newcomer but will swear it is a dozen. The wail is the strangest, weirdest, most baffling sound known to any wilderness—a wild medley of bark, howl, shriek, and whine utterly confounding; and as to its articulation, glib as nothing else I know.

—CHARLES F. LUMMIS
southern Texas
c. 1898

SIDEWAYS TRUTHS

I was born in Rhode Island, you know, and it got too little for me. When I lay down, my head would like as not be in the lap of somebody in Massachusetts and my feet bothering somebody else in Connecticut. I just got too big for the state, so I thought Texas would be big enough for me.

—SHANGHAI PIERCE
Texas panhandle
1900

I was raised in a canebrake by an old mama lion.
I got a head like a bombshell and teeth made of iron.
I got nine rows of jaw teeth, and holes punched for more.
I come from ourang-a-tang, where the bullfrogs taught me
to snore.

—ANONYMOUS

I'm a wild wolf, and I'm gonna eat meat alive. I'm a wild wolf, and my tail never touched the ground.

—ANONYMOUS

Last summer I wauz ridin' along thinkin' as how the weather must be hotter'n Satan in long handles, when i hears a low moanin' behind me and turns 'round to see a blizzard whizzin' in. Right away I knows I got no time for admirin' the scenery, so I jabs steel an' heads for home. That ol' hoss musta known about blizzards, too, 'cause 'fore I had time t' chaw my terbaccer twice, we wuz there. But when I went to unsaddle the animal, danged if I didn't find its frequarters plum' foamy with sweat and its hindquarters frozen solid with ice where th' teeth of the blizzard had caught it.

—J. FRANK DOBIE
Dallas, Texas
1936

It got so derned cold at our ranch one winter that the thermometer dropped to ninety-five degrees below zero. Our foreman came out to give us orders fer the day, but the words froze as they came out of his mouth. We had to break 'em off one by one so's we could tell what he was sayin'.

—ANONYMOUS COWBOY
quoted in *Life* magazine
1942

First cowboy: I did own an ol' hoss one time that was about the *dumbest* critter I ever did see. I'll tell yuh what that fool horse did one night when I drunk too much likker and passed out in town. He picked me up and slung me on his back and carred me twenty miles to the ranch. When he got me there, he pulled off my boots with his teeth and nosed me into my bunk. Then he went to the kitchen, fixed up a pot of coffee, and brung me a cup all fixed up with cream and sugar. Then the next day I had a hangover, and he went by hisself and dug post holes all day so's the boss would let me sleep. When I woke up and found out what that fool hoss had done, I cussed him for two days without stoppin' and wished him off on a greener which was passin' by. It wuz good riddance, too.

Second cowboy: I'd say that wuz a pretty smart horse. What in the world did you get rid of him for?

First cowboy: Smart, heck! Who ever heard of a real cowboy usin' cream and sugar in his coffee?

—*Arizona Nights*
by STEWART EDWARD WHITE
1907

TRAIL'S END

I drove over every trail from the Gulf of Mexico to the Dakotas and Montana, but the Chisholm Trail was the one I traveled most. Now, after thirty years of settled life, the call of the trail is with me still, and there is not a day that I do not long to mount my horse and be out among the cattle.

—L. B. ANDERSON
Seguin, Texas
c. 1920

I put in eighteen or twenty years on the trail, and all I had in the final outcome was the high-heeled boots, the striped pants, and about $4.80 worth of other clothes, so there you are.

—G. O. Burrows
Del Rio, Texas
c. 1920

TOM MIX'S TRAIL FAREWELL

May you brand your largest calf crop,
May your range grass never fail,
May your water holes stay open,
May you ride an easy trail;
May you never reach for leather
Nor your saddle horse go lame;
May you drop your loop on critters
With your old unerring aim.
May your stack of chips grow taller,
May your shootin' e'er stay true,
May good luck plumb snow you under—
Is always my wish for you.

—Tom Mix

3

LOVE & HORSES

I've often said there's nothing better for the inside of a man than the outside of a horse.

—RONALD REAGAN

Not a day's gone by that I wouldn't rather have been with my horse than with people.

—Luke Perry
Hollywood, California
star of *8 Seconds*
1994

No Creature on Earth is more noble, more patient, more obedient, and more, plain old helpful than a good Horse, well broke by a man who loves her dear. On a hot day in the middle of no-place, she's also the best-looking gal anywhere, and if they made bride's gowns to fit a Paint horse, I'd soon marry the horse as a woman but I don't know a horse who would have me.

—OLIVER CURTIS
El Paso, Texas
1912

Let me dispose right now of a malicious rumor that has haunted me all my life: I did not kiss my horse! We may have nuzzled a little, but we never kissed. *Never*.

I can take a joke, but it bothered ol' Champ.

—GENE AUTRY

Cowboys hate walking: They really know how to use their horses. They conserve the energy of the horse, treating it like a valuable piece of farm equipment. They seldom ride all out, contrary to many dudes' visions of what riding the range is all about. Cowboying requires real knowledge of a horse and his capabilities. A horse can sense when a real horseman is in the saddle. He knows when the rider is going to tough it out.

—ROBERT REDFORD
Hole-in-the-Wall, Wyoming
1975

I keep a secret as well as the next man, but I tell my horse everything. I mean *everything*. Even secrets I would never tell my wife. Even secrets I'd never tell another man's wife, for that matter.

—STEW STEWART
Truro, Alberta, Canada
1956

"Horse talk" is a low grunt which seems to charm a horse and make him stand perfectly still for a moment or so at a time. It sounds like "hoh-hoh," uttered deep down in one's chest. The horse will stop his rough antics and strain motionless on the rope for a few seconds; while he is doing this and looking straight at the approaching figure, the man will wave a blanket at him and hiss at him—"Shuh! Shuh!" It takes about fifteen minutes of this to make the horse realize that the man is harmless; that no motion which he makes, no sound that he utters, will harm him in any way.

—CHIEF BUFFALO CHILD LONG LANCE
Cardston, Alberta, Canada
1928

A man on foot is no man at all.

—ANONYMOUS

HORSE SWAPPING

Cattlemen were constantly selling horses to each other, and when a horse changed hands it was likely to take the name of its former owner. I have heard cowpunchers make remarks as these: "Catch John Blocker for Juan," "Dillard Fant is lame," "Clabe Merchant has a sore back," "Bill Reed broke his rope last night," "Mark Withers kicked the cook," "The dadblamed Indians stole Shanghai Pierce and George West last night."

—GEORGE SAUNDERS
founder, Texas Trail Drivers Association
San Antonio, Texas
c. 1925

If you want to find horses, go to the prettiest place in reach, and there you'll almost always find them. Horses love beauty as much as humans do.

—EUGENE MANLOVE RHODES
Bar Cross Ranch, New Mexico
1930

If you have a horse with four white legs,
Keep him not a day; if you have a horse with three white legs,
Send him far away; if you have a horse with two white legs,
Sell him to a friend; if you have a horse with one white leg,
Keep him to the end.

> —Captain John G. Bourke
> 5th Cavalry, U.S.A.
> 1876

A good horse is never a bad color.

> —Anonymous

The quarterhorse tends to be the favorite of cowboys and ranchers now. I don't think that was always true—my father loved Morgans and some people like Appaloosas, which are really workmanlike, and they tend to be calm horses. Quarterhorses are good at working with cattle because they're quick; they make good cutting horses. They're bred for that. We had some Arabians when I was younger, but they were too hot—they had lots of energy and endurance, so even after you rode one all day, he would still have enough energy to buck you off.

—CYD MCMULLEN
Elko, Nevada
1993

It sure helps if you know you've got a good horse. The first time I met Trigger, I wanted to know how good a horse he was, so I got on him and turned him. Well, he could spin on a dime and give you nine cents back in change. We just fell in love. From then on, I never let him out of my sight. Finding a horse like Trigger is like finding a wife. The horse is your other half in this—he's your partner, and he can get you out of plenty of scrapes and close calls.

—ROY ROGERS

In Texas, the history of the horse is equally as important as that of its owner.

—ANONYMOUS
in *The Daughter of Texas*
1886

OPERATING INSTRUCTIONS

You git on a horse from the left and off the same way. Some folks leave by a different door, but that's because they forgot to git hold of the steering wheel, which is the reins. The first thing a man should know about a horse is that the reins is everything—brakes, starter, steering—everything. The stirrups give you something to stand up on when the ride gets a little rough, and the saddle horn, it'll give you a place to tie off a steer or what have you. But a cowboy without reins is a man just waiting to hit something hard.

—LEWIS ELIAS
Montana
1931

If I'm going to get on a horse that someone else has saddled up, before I get on I'm going to check out the cinch and the blanket beneath the saddle. If the blanket is not on right, it can rub the horse's hair the wrong direction and give him saddle sores. Then, you check the cinch. To do that, you make sure you can get two fingers between the strap and the horse's belly. The last thing I would look at is the bit—you want to be sure that it's not too tight or too loose for the horse. Usually, I offer to saddle up my horse for myself.

—SHANA ZUCKER
Pinole, California
1993

When your ass hurts more than your legs, that's when you've got your stirrups adjusted to the right length. Some people say you should stand beside the horse and your stirrups should end at the bottom of your armpit, but the bottom line is, you want to be able to stand up in the stirrups a little bit—you want to be able to clear about two inches under your crotch when you stand in them.

—BRUCE NEGRE
Fresno, California
1994

It is the roper's horse that can really make or break a champion. Keep your eye on that cow pony when the chute opens and the calf breaks into a dead run in front of him. It's the spectacular speed of the horse that gives the rider a chance to sling that rope out and encircle the calf's head—and it's the action of the horse in keeping the rope taunt after the catch, that helps the rider make "time." Two throws are allowed before the rider is disqualified. The rider dismounts the instant the catch is made, leaving the rope tied to the saddle horn. At this point, it's the horse's job to keep the rope just tight enough by backing away or moving forward, always facing the calf until the tie is made. Three of the calf's feet must be securely tied with the piggin string. It's "no time" for the cowboy if the calf can get up after it is tied.

—MAX KEGLEY
Phoenix, Arizona
1942

HOW TO MAKE A QUICK GETAWAY

Sometimes it just happens where you're standing over here, and your horse is over there, and there's a whole heck of a lot of big trouble in between. What you want in the worst way is to get to your horse, make a running mount, and clear out before the bullets start to fly.

To do a running mount:

1. Run alongside your horse with both hands on the saddle horn. Then, as the horse picks up speed, but before he reaches a gallop, you kick your feet forward to a point alongside about where his front feet are. Plant your heels. Then, what with the momentum of the horse, you bounce up into the saddle, just like that.

2. Land in the saddle. As you jump, the horse's about in the right position for you to swing your right leg over the saddle. This does take a little arm strength, of course, but not all that much. It's not as bad as doing a pull-up, even. But you have to have enough strength to be able to keep yourself from going past the saddle and ending up on the far side of the horse.

3. Grab the reins before you put your feet in the stirrups. You ought to leave the reins around the horse's neck, where

you can reach them easily. As you get better at this, you'll do all three—land in the saddle, grab the reins, get your feet in the stirrups—all at about the same time. But that's the order, in case something goes wrong.

If you don't get this right the first time, you'll have a mighty powerful incentive to improve. You'll only miss that saddle three or four times before you get pretty accurate. I always find that experience is a swell teacher with something like this.

—ROY ROGER

MUSTANG MANIA

If ever there was a horse paradise, it was this staked plain of Texas, and here the mustangs were in all their glory—tens of thousands of them. I have heard the number put as high as fifty thousand, and I believe that was a low estimate. These horses were well grown, larger than the mustangs in south Texas, fourteen to fifteen hands high. Some of the stallions were over fifteen hands and weighed 1,000 to 1,100 pounds.

—FRANK COLLINSON
El Paso, Texas
c. 1936

The wild horse can see, hear, and smell a man farther than any other animal, except a woman.

—FRANK M. LOCKARD
Norton, Kansas
1924

[When chasing mustangs] the rider had better not be riding a plug draft horse if he expects to keep within the dust. The rider should change horses as often as possible and riders should be relieved as often as convenient. After four or five days of about seventy-five miles per day, the horses become tired and will let the rider come within two hundred yards of them.

The first horse caught should be the stallion with the largest harem. Then his harem should all be caught and put with him, when all the herd have been clogged, except the yearlings and two-year-olds, and some of the weaker ones. The herd is brought to within fifty yards of the tent door at sunrise and kept there until noon. Then the man in charge will whistle to them and start them toward the lake to drink and graze for one hour and a half. He then brings them back to the same place to stand until sundown, when they are started to the lake to spend the night. This procedure is repeated every day, the reason being that if the horses graze all day, they will wander away at night. But if they are kept hungry all day, they will graze at night and not be far away in the morning.

—HOMER HOYT
Greeley, Colorado
1934

Nothing scares a horse quicker than a quiet thing that moves toward him and makes no noise. He will jump and break his neck at a noisy movement of a rodent in the grass or a falling twig, while a roaring buffalo or a steaming train will pass him unnoticed. That is because he has the same kind of courage that man has: Real courage, the courage to face any odds that he can see and hear and cope with, but a superstitious fear of anything ghostlike.

—CHIEF BUFFALO CHILD LONG LANCE
Cardston, Alberta, Canada
1928

The first act in breaking a horse is to catch him. In the early days this was done by penning the *manada*, the bunch of mares, with which the young, unbroken horses ran, then roping the *potro*—the unbroken horse—that had been selected. If there were a choice, the selection would be of a *potro* about five years old. Any horse younger than this lacked the strength and endurance to do the hard work that might be required of him; older than this, the horse would be harder to break.

—RUTH DODSON
Mathis, Texas
c. 1940

When you go to ride a bad horse, first get your horse by the bridle and pull his head to one side as far as you can and stick your five fingers in his eyes as deep as you can and if the horse pitches, sit as limber as you can and twist your toes around in your saddle stirrup and you will find that it will be much easier on you and always handle stubborn horses rough and use limber bits and make him go your way and not his.

—LONDON BROWN
Nocona, Texas
1892

My granddad taught me how to fall from a horse: When you hit the ground, you curl. He said, "There will come a time when you're going to get bucked, and you're going to need to know what to do so you don't get stepped on." And you do that by curling in; you get your arms and legs in real close to your body—unless you feel like waving 'em around out there in front of the horse like a target.

—Valerie Farmer
Shreveport, Louisiana
1994

There are more horses' asses in the world than there are horses.
—Gage Lovett Martin
1964

THE NAMES OF THE BEASTS

The cowboy's usually the one on top.

Cowboy	Hoss
Ken Maynard	Tarzan
Hoot Gibson	Mutt
Lone Ranger	Silver
Hoppy	Topper
Tim McCoy	Midnight
Lash LaRue	Rush
Cisco Kid	Diablo
Tonto	Scout
Rex Allen	Ko-Ko
Johnny Mack Brown	Rebel
Smiley Burdette	Ring Eye
Roy	Trigger
Dale	Buttermilk
Gene	Champion

—*Way Out West*
by JANE and MICHAEL STERN
1993
and my AUNT CANDY
1994

4

LOVE & WOMEN

When Roy dies, I'm going to have him stuffed and mounted on top of Trigger.

—DALE EVANS

Jealousy's a funny thing with women. A man gets jealous, he gets right to the bottom of it. He screams, yells, shoots, whatever it takes to clear the air. But a woman, she just stews and plots and waits. It's almost enough to scare a man onto the straight and narrow.

—JACK MCMAHON
Casper, Wyoming
1946

I fell in love with a very beautiful woman and married her, but I was tortured by the fear that she was unfaithful to me; so one day, in order to satisfy my doubts, I told her that I would visit my parents in Magdalena.

That evening I went down and took the train, but at the first station I got off and walked back to my house. Sure enough, there was a light in my wife's bedroom and in great excitement I crept up and looked through the keyhole. But some clothes were hung over a chair in front of it and I could not see. Neither could I see through the crack of the door.

I thought then of looking through the transom, but as you see I am a very short man and, as there was nothing for me to stand on, I took out this eye and held it up to the transom. There, instead of another man, I beheld my poor wife sitting upon the bed and weeping over my picture. This so agitated me that I ran from the house and clear to the railroad station, resolved that she should never know of my suspicions. But in my excitement I still carried my eye in my hand, and when I reached the station it was so cold and had swelled up so that I could never get it back in.

—EL TUERTO

There was an unwritten law, recognized by the good women of the towns as well as of the country, that whenever a party of cow hunters rode up and asked to have bread baked, it mattered not the time of day, the request was to be cheerfully complied with. Not from fear of insult in case of refusal—for each and every cowboy was the champion defender of womanhood, and would have scorned to have uttered a disrespectful word in her presence—but from an accommodating spirit and a kindness of heart which was universally characteristic in those frontier days. I remember the many times that cow hunters rode up to my father's house, and, telling my mother they were out of bread, asked that she would kindly bake their flour for them. Everything was at once made ready. The sack was lifted from the pack horse and brought in, and in due time the bread wallets were once more filled with freshly cooked biscuit, and the cowboys rode away with grateful appreciation. These acts of consideration on the part of my mother were entirely gratuitous, but the generous-hearted cowboys would always leave either a half-sack of flour or a money donation as a free-will offering.

—LUTHER A. LAWHON
San Antonio, Texas
c. 1920

Being the only woman in camp, the men rivaled each other in attentiveness to me. They were always on the lookout for something to please me, a surprise of some delicacy of the wild fruit, or prairie chicken, or antelope tongue.

—Mrs. Amanda Burks
Cotulla, Texas
c. 1920

At every stopping place, the men made little fires in their frying pans, and set them around me, to keep off the mosquitos while I took my meal. As the columns of smoke rose about me, I felt like a heathen goddess to whom incense was being offered.

—Caroline Leighton
en route to Puget Sound
c. 1884

Get down there and pick it up, you ignorant bastard. Haven't you got any manners when you're with ladies?

—BELLE STARR
to her husband, Blue Duck,
after losing her hat to a gust of wind
Fort Smith, Oklahoma Territory
c. 1875

COWPOKE COURTSHIP

I saw how a man meets his wife, this was in Oklahoma at a legion dance. The feller was standin' with me and the boys talkin' about horses mostly but also wimmin a little bit. There was a new girl in town from Texas I think or from Loosianna and all the girls was watchin' out for her but she knew what she wanted, that feller. She walked over to him and smiled and when he smiled back she stuck a hook in the corner of his mouth. He didn't feel a thing, he didn't even see it go in. So then she went back over to the bench where her girlfriends were sitting waiting for us gents to call on them for a dance. After that she didn't do much except smile and slowly reel the feller in until he was wagglin' and thrashin' around on her bank, wondering what worm did he swallow and when. Now they have four boys and a half-section.

—ELMER FITCH
Northbranch, Kansas
1933

You must go down to the stream at twilight, sit on the bank, and wait for my niece to come down and fetch water. You will find other young men waiting for her, and probably one or two of them will jump up and throw their blankets over her head and talk to her. You must watch, and when you see the first sent away by her, and the second, and perhaps also the third, you will try your luck. I am inclined to think you will succeed where others have failed. When you have thrown your blanket well over her head, and popped your own beneath it, you can tell her all, and I will answer for it she will listen. You can tell her you love her, that you admire her, and that if she will marry you, you will give her every comfort and necessary—in fact, tell her all the nonsense young men tell girls when they want to marry. You will go down to the stream, go through the same performance, repeat the same words, every evening for ten evenings. At the end of that time, you will return to me and report the result. Go now, my son; I do not wish to speak to you on the subject until then, so be good enough not to refer to it again.

—CHIEF SPOTTED TAIL's instructions to
John Young Nelson on the proper methodology
for courting his niece, Wom-bel-ee-zee-zee
Platte River, Nebraska
1843

I never thought I'd marry anybody but a cowboy. Maybe that's why I'm still not married.

—ROSIE
northern Nevada
c. 1990

Nothing men do surprises me. I'm ready for them. I know how to whack below the belt.

—PATSY CLINE
Nashville
1960

Sunday, May 24, 1840. Rested well last night. Awoke about 4 o'clock a.m. Rather restless. Arose at 5. Helped about milking. But by the time I had done that found it necessary to call my husband & soon the Dr. I had scarcely time to dress & comb my hair before I was too sick to do it. Before eight was delivered of a fine daughter with far less suffering than the birth of our son. The morning was pleasant. In the p.m. fine thunder shower. Babe very quiet. Think it weighs not more than eight pounds.... Have been reading Mrs. Trollopes Domestic Manual of the Americans the past two weeks, find her disgustingly interesting.

—MARY WALKER
Waiilattu, Oregon
1840

No English gals for me. Give me a Kentucky gal or a Texas gal or a Kansas gal every time, a gal who knows how to cook ol' corn bread and make good coffee. What them English gals want? Tea and white bread all the time. Where you all gonna find tea and white bread in a cow camp?

—GUS WHITE
Wheeler County, Texas
c. 1880

Our furniture consisted of a pioneer bed, made by boring three holes in the logs of the wall in one corner, in which to drive the rails. Thus the bedstead required but one leg. The table was a mere rough shelf, fastened to the wall, and supported by two legs. Three smaller shelves answered for a cupboard, and were amply sufficient for my slender supply of dishes, which comprised mostly tinware, which, in those days, was kept scrupulously bright and shining. My sugar bowl, cream jug, steel knives and forks (two-tined), and one set of German silver teaspoons, I had bought with my own little savings before my marriage.

—Bethenia Owens
Roseburg, Oregon
c. 1854

It has been said of the cowboy that he feared only two things—
the hospital and a woman. There were only a few women in the
cow country. Not more than one-half of the homes upon the
range had a woman in them. The women who were there had
not alone the protection of law—a feeble thing—but the protection of men. You might neglect, mistreat, or even steal a man's
stock, and get by with it; but *caramba*! Let his woman alone.

—OSCAR RUSH
Salt Lake City, Utah
1930

The old-time cowboy was most respectful of women as long
as they kept their place. If they let down the bars, one of those
boys would go the limit.

—OLIVER WALLIS
Laramie, Wyoming
c. 1950

A cowboy is pretty touchy in protecting a woman's character. He feels that a man is pretty low that would bring a woman into contact with dirt, or allow her to touch it of her own accord. He places her on a high fence because he wants to look up to her. He wants her feminine with frills and fluffs all over. He has no use for those he-women who wear pants and try to dress like a man.

—RAMON ADAMS
Sonoma, Texas
1969

W*anted:* A nice, plump, healthy, good-natured, good-looking, domestic and affectionate lady to correspond with. Object—matrimony. She must be between 22 and 35 years of age. She must be a believer in God and immortality, but no sectarian. She must not be a gadabout or given to scandal, but must be one who will be a help-mate and companion, and who will endeavor to make home happy. Such a lady can find a correspondent by addressing the editor of this paper. Photographs exchanged!

If anybody don't like our way of going about this interesting business, we don't care. It's none of their funeral.

—Notice in the *Yuma Sentinel*
Yuma, Arizona
1875

THE DISCOVERY OF UNDERWEAR

We met a couple of "upper ten" ladies of Iowa City dressed out and out Bloomer style, black cassimere pants and black cloth coats, high heel boots, finished off with a low crown black hat—I think Duey and I followed them about three squares before our curiosity was satisfied.

—DAVID SPAIN
Iowa City, Iowa
1859

The Bloomer was an uncouth being, her hair, cut level with her eyes, depended with the graceful curve of a drake's tail around the flat Turanian countenance, whose only expression was sullen insolence. The body-dress, glazed brown calico, fitted her somewhat like a soldier's tunic, developing haunches which would be admired only in venison.

—SIR RICHARD BURTON
Horseshoe Station, Wyoming
1860

We bedded our cattle for the last time near Abilene, Kansas. The boss let myself and another boy go to the city one day, so we went into town, tied our ponies, and the first place we visited was a saloon and dance hall. We ordered toddies like we had seen older men do, and drank them down, for we were dry, very dry, as it had been a long ways between drinks. I quit my partner, as he had a girl to talk to, so I went out and in a very short time I went into another store and saloon. I got another toddy, my hat began to stiffen up, but I pushed it up in front, moved my pistol to where it would be handy, then sat down on a box in the saloon and picked up a newspaper and thought I would read a few lines, but my two toddies were at war, so I could not very well understand what I read. I got up and left for more sights—you have seen them in Abilene, Dodge City, and any other places those days. I walked around for perhaps an hour. The two toddies were making me feel different to what I had felt for months, and I thought it was about time for another, so I headed for a place across the street, where I could hear a fiddle. It was a saloon, gambling and dancing hall. I went to the bar and called for a toddy, and as I was drinking it a girl came up and put her little hand under my chin and looked me square in the face and said, "Oh, you pretty Texas boy, give me a drink." I asked her what she wanted and she said anything I took, so I called for two toddies. My, I was getting rich fast—a pretty girl and plenty of whiskey.

—J. L. McCaleb
Carrizo Springs, Texas
c. 1920

I've laid it in all of 'em [towns]. I throwed my fannie twenty-one times a night, five bucks a throw, and by the time old red-eye come up, I was eatin' breakfast drunker'n an Indian.

—Anonymous
Oklahoma panhandle
c. 1900

We drove cattle for a month, then rolled into town and there learned two important things about dance-hall gals. Firstly, the longer you have been gone, the better it looks. Second, the better it looks, the more it costs.

—Willis Barnes
Chicago
1938

5

WOMEN & GUNS

WHAT A COWGIRL NEEDS TO KNOW ABOUT MEN AND GUNS:

1. Strange men will do for you to shoot; or you can scare them to death.

2. Shoot first, ask questions later.

3. If you shoot a man in the back, he rarely has a chance to return fire.

4. Shoot from ambush if possible.

5. If a man needs killing, go ahead and do it, especially if there is no one you can consult about it.

—MRS. FRANK ADAMS
c. 1900
quoted by Joyce Gibson Roach
in *The West That Was*

Dear Lewis,

The Apaches came. I'm mighty nigh out of buckshot. Please send more.

Your loving wife.

—MRS. LEWIS STEVENS's
message to her husband after repelling an Indian attack
Lonesome Valley, Arizona
c. 1874

I shot Mr. Baldwin even though we are related by blood. He ruined me in body and mind.

—VERONA BALDWIN
alleged cousin of Lucky Baldwin
San Francisco
c. 1890

Men sometimes need little reminders. Many's a time when I tied a string around a man's finger to help him remember his way home, and every now and then a loaded pistol does wonders to restore a man's memory of good manners toward women.

—LOUISE BALLCOTT
Harmony, Oklahoma
1883

The hotels were overflowing, but the proprietor of one small place agreed to house [Pete] in a room with another guest, provided the consent of the first guest could be secured. This was easily done and the two shared a double bed. Pete and the roommate talked of many things, among them Belle Starr and her escapades. During the conversation, Pete entertained a keen desire to meet this famous Western woman.

The next morning, Pete found that the other guest had risen before him. When he went down to the veranda, a fine horse stood saddled at the rack. His roommate came out and mounted.

"Did you say you'd like to see Belle Starr?" he asked.

"Yes."

"Well," said the other, turning to gallop away, "you slept with her last night."

—MODY C. BOATWRIGHT
Dallas, Texas
c. 1934

Now look-a-here, young fellow, you look honest and smart. You come up to Deadwood with me, and start practicin' and if there isn't enough law business to begin with I'll make it for you.

—CALAMITY JANE
to a young lawyer encountered on a train
1877

THE OAKLEY METHOD OF SHOOTING SKEET

You don't sight them. You just swing with them, and when it feels right, pull.

—ANNIE OAKLEY
Darke Country, Ohio
c. 1890

I was eight years old when I made my first shot, and I still consider it one of the best shots I ever made. I saw a squirrel run down over the grass in front of the house, through the orchard and stop on the fence to get a hickory nut. I decided to shoot it and ran into the house to get a gun which was hanging on the wall and which I knew to be loaded. I was so little I had to jump up on a chair and slide it down to the mantel and then to the ground. I laid the gun on the railing of the porch, and then recalled that I had heard my brother say about shooting: "It is a disgrace to shoot a squirrel anywhere but in the head because it spoils the meat to hit him else-where." I took the remark literally and decided, in a flash, that I must hit that squirrel in the head, or be disgraced. It was a wonderful shot, going right through the head from side to side. My mother was so frightened when she learned that I had taken down the loaded gun and shot it that I was forbidden to touch it again for eight months.

—ANNIE OAKLEY
in *Philadelphia Public Ledger*
1919

"You cain't shoot a man in the tail like a quail."

—ANNIE OAKLEY
according to Rogers and Hammerstein's
Annie Get Your Gun
1947

6

GREENHORNS, TENDERFEET, & OTHER AMUSEMENTS

The funniest sight in the world to a veteran cowhand was a greenhorn who had suffered a sprained ankle or dislocated shoulder from falling off his horse.

—WILLIAM H. FORBIS
Bozeman, Montana
1973

There was once this man from back East who thought he would fancy the life of a cowpoke, so he joined up for a cattle drive. The first night, as the men were bedding down, someone tossed the man a piece of wood. "Here, enjoy this," he said. "Tomorrow we're hitting the plains and you cain't git no kind of pillow out there." They say the fellow gave up and went home the next day.

—ANONYMOUS

30 miles to water
20 miles to wood
10 inches to Hell
Gone Back East to Wife's family
            —Sign found on the door of an abandoned shack
                                    Texas panhandle
                                        c. 1910

A tenderfoot, a regular softie greenhorn, come out from the East. I was dealin' at a little minin' joint called White Bonanza in Colorado. This tenderfoot sat in the game, and he lost from the first turn.

"I say, you know," he blurts out, "you must be cheating!"

Well, if it hadn't been for his blamed Eastern accent, I'd ha' shot him without thinkin'. As it was, everyone ducked. I jest looked at him and said, "Young man, that means shootin' out here."

He got pretty white and said, "I—I didn't mean any harm, but when you get a man's money and he hasn't any opportunity to get it back, it looks queer, don't you know? After all, old chap, gambling is cheating."

The rest o' the boys began to hustle him away, but I stopped 'em, an' made him explain. He didn't know any more about monty than a hog does about a side-saddle, but he could argufy the spots off'n the cards. After he got through, I sat a-thinkin'.

"Boys," I said, "this kid is right, though he don't know which end of a gun to load. I'm a-goin' to earn money after this."

One o' the boys, who had a claim that hadn't panned out any too good, though there was pay dirt in it, sung out, "I'll trade you, sight unseen, my claim for what you got in the bank and yo'r lay-out."

"You're covered," says I, and I ain't never bet a cent on a card from that day to this.

—SHANE RYDER
Abilene, Kansas
1869

Early in the spring of 1882 I was employed by a Mark Withers of Lockhart, to go up the trail with a herd to Kansas. I was pretty much of a "tenderfoot," just a slip of a boy, and the hands told me [another rider named] Hill was a pretty tough character and would steal anything he could get his hands on, besides he might kill me if I didn't watch him. They loaded me up pretty well on this kind of information, and I really believed it. They would steal my matches, cartridges, cigarette papers, and handkerchiefs, and tell me that Hill got them. I reached the time when I was deprived of almost everything I had and even had to skin prickly pears to get wrapping for my cigarettes, believing all the while that the fellow Hill had cleaned me up. Things were getting serious and I was desperate, and if Hill made any kind of a break the consequences would have probably been disaster. At last Hill, who was fully aware of the game that was being played on me, called me aside and told me that it was all a put-up job, and said it had been carried far enough. We all had a good laugh and from that time forward harmony reined in camp.

—HENRY D. STEELE
San Antonio, Texas
1920

The first day in the saddle on the open range was a tough one on the tenderfoot. The easiest saddle on the rider in the world once you are used to it, the cow saddle is far harder to get on comfortable terms with than the flat pigskin; it gives a beginner harder cramps and tender spots on more parts of the anatomy than any punishment conceivable short of an inquisition rack.

—EDGAR BEECHER BRONSON
New York City
1910

The ranch foreman, on welcoming Mr. New Yorker, a visitor, would say something like the following: "Mr. New Yorker, shake hands with Hen. Hen, this is Mr. New Yorker from back East. He's a friend of the boss. Mr. New Yorker, Hen's been with our outfit for six years, and is generally reckoned to be the slickest rider in this half of the country."

If, after Hen had passed beyond earshot, Mr. New Yorker had asked the foreman for Hen's last name, the questioner would have seen a look of sudden surprise, and would have heard: "Well, I'll be damned. I never thought of that. He likely has got one somewhere. I dunno what it is. He's just Hen, and if he thinks that's good enough for him, it shore is for us, and that's about the size of it. Say, stranger, let me give you some advice: If I were you I wouldn't try to hurry nothin', and I'd travel on the idea that Hen likely gave a first-class funeral to the rest of his names, and I wouldn't ask him for no resurrections."

—PHILIP ASHTON ROLLINS
Cheyenne, Wyoming
1922

Soon as the newness wears off, [greenhorns] quit and go back with the idea that they know all about this—that there's no more to learn—when at the same time they haven't started to know at all, and are just as helpless as ever. Some folks have an idea that you can qualify to be an all around good cowhand in a couple of years, and where they get that idea, I don't know.

—FOREMAN
Three Rivers Cattle Company, Montana
1902

RISKY BUSINESS

I am going to say something about the great American game—draw poker. It stands alone, in a class by itself. If it have a peer, 'tis the game of life. Life itself is but a gamble. I am not a gambler, but most real cowmen or punchers I ever knew could play good enough to lose.

—OSCAR RUSH
Salt Lake City, Utah
1930

I'm buyin' a round of drinks an' supper for the whole crowd. An' if anybody present reckons he can play poker he's goin' to need a barrel to get home in.

—HOPALONG CASSIDY

RODEO

It takes a lot of courage for a man to pay out his dollar to enter a rodeo and then, after not winning a red cent, walk away saying, "Sure lucky I didn't get hurt."

—HOOT GIBSON
Hollywood, California
1912

The rules of the sport are simple. As soon as the steer leaves the chute, it is followed by the wrestler and the hazer, the latter's object being to prevent it dodging away from the wrestler's horse.

As the wrestler approaches the steer, he leans sideways in the saddle ready to throw himself on its shoulders and grasp it by the horns. The faster the pace, the easier it is to obtain a grip quickly—the most difficult steers being those which will not gallop and allow the horses to outstrip them. Once the wrestler has flung himself out of the saddle—some literally dive forward, being clear of the horse before they touch the steer—his immediate object is to use his legs as a brake, while grasping the animal by its horns, and bring it to a stand. Sometimes the man will be dragged half across the ground before he can attempt the throw. Sometimes—and this is one of the greatest risks—the steer will overbalance on account of the man's weight and the pace, turning a complete somersault. This is called "hoolihaning" a steer and does not count as a throw. Occasionally the wrestler fails to obtain a hold and falls under the steer and the galloping horses. But as a rule the man is very sure of his grip; the animal is pulled up, and with every second counting in his chances of a prize the wrestler uses the leverage of the horns, obtaining a scientific lock, and if he is lucky twists the animal over, bringing it down on its side and raising a hand as signal to the judges. The time of the record throw is seven seconds, counted from the moment the steer crosses the white line opposite the chute.

—R. B. CUNNINGHAME GRAHAM
London
1936

BUSTIN' BRONCS

We would have lots of fun trying to prove who was the best rider, but oftentimes the horse would prove that he was onto his job better than any of us.

—F. M. POLK
Luling, Texas
c. 1920

Being a rodeo rider is a state of mind. It is for yourself—your self-esteem, pride and ego. You're brainwashed at an early age to want to emulate your heroes. You always want to be like them. For a lot of kids, myself included, cowboys are the last real heroes.

—CHRIS LEDOUX
Kaycee, Wyoming
1994

I was a saddle-bronc rider, and here's how it worked: They bring the animal in, I would put my saddle on it, and that animal and I would be physically connected for eight seconds, and if I won I'd get my paycheck, get in my car and go on to the next rodeo. The eight seconds is the time that everyone has to ride; you have to ride for eight seconds or you are disqualified. If you get bumped off before that, you are disqualified. If you touch the animal with your free hand, you are disqualified. If you don't have your spurs in a certain position when the ride starts, you are disqualified. If you do all that, then they start giving you points and the man who gets the most points gets the most money. Then you're in your car and down the road going to the next rodeo.

—DON FARMER
Elko, Nevada
1994

Keep your jewels clear!

—STEPHEN BALDWIN
Hollywood, California
costar of *8 Seconds*
1994

It takes plenty of nerve to come out of the chutes aloft a plunging bundle of dynamite with hooves; and it takes plenty of riding ability to stay on for ten seconds (the required length of the ride). There's more to it than just staying on, too. The horse must come out bucking, or the rider gets a mount that will. Rider must come out of the chutes spurring, with blunt spurs, high on the shoulders, and continue to spur from the shoulders back to flank throughout the ride. Both feet must be kept in the stirrups. The rein must be held in one hand, not wrapped around, and the other hand must be kept in the air, and must not touch the bronc, the rider, or the saddle! The contestant must use a committee saddle and halter, but he furnishes his own rein, chaps, and spurs.

—MAX KEGLEY
Phoenix, Arizona
1942

MARK TWAIN'S DANCING LESSON

The dancers are formed in two long ranks, facing each other, and the battle opens with some light skirmishing between the pickets, which is gradually resolved into a general engagement along the whole line; after that you have nothing to do but stand by and grab every lady that drifts within reach of you, and swing her. It is very entertaining, and elaborately scientific also.

—SAMUEL CLEMENS
in *The Territorial Enterprise*
Virginia City, Nevada
c. 1862

NEWS

The individual who left three kittens, and a dog with a tin pan tied to his narrative, on our office stairs last night, can have them in a transfigured state by calling at the butcher shop. We would modestly suggest that we have no further call for such supplies.

—*The Daily Monitor*
Fort Scott, Kansas
1870

It's an awful good feeling to feel that you are the only man in a town of three thousand people whose liver don't kick the breath out of him every time a stranger comes along and takes a good look at the bridge of your nose.

—SAMUEL STOREY
in *To the Gold Land*
1889

Some woman is always found to be an accomplice in all such scrapes, and we think they ought to be banished from the community.

—*The Daily Monitor*
Fort Scott, Kansas
reporting an 1872 suicide

A large, broad-shouldered, bulldog head, short-haired man, is wanted immediately at this office, to serve as fighting editor for the Sentinel. Applicants will please send weight—whether light or heavy—also the number of men he has "chawed up." Terms—half the profits.

—Want ad in the Yuma *Sentinel*
October 5, 1872

A COWBOY JOKE

Two cowpokes had punched cattle together for years, and one time they were out on a long haul. Each day, the two men would get up, ride off in different directions to corral the herd, and at the end of the day's trek, they'd cook dinner and go to sleep. Day after day this continued. One night as they were about to fall off to sleep they heard a bellowing noise coming from the cattle.

"Bull," said the first one.

"Sounds like a steer to me," said the other.

The next day, the two men delivered the cattle to their destination and the first cowboy saddled up his horse to depart.

"Leaving?" asked the other cowboy.

"Yep," said the first. "Too much damned argument."

—Anonymous

7
TROUBLE

They'll have to shoot me first to take my gun.

—ROY ROGERS

If they start takin' away guns, they're gonna have to back me up against a wall and that's no lie.

—CURT TAYLOR
Blue Creek Ranch, Wyoming
1975

When old age really gets its rope onto you, you can shift to a .38, then to a .32, an' fall back on a single-shot .22. If yo're still alive after that, an' gettin' weaker, I'll buy you one of them silver-plated air rifles.

—HOPALONG CASSIDY

Shoot 'em up Joe.
Run for sheriff 1872.
Run from sheriff 1876
Buried 1876.

—Boot Hill epitaph
Dodge City, Kansas

GALLOWS HUMOR

Every man for his principles. Hurrah for Jeff Davis. Let 'er go, men!

—Boone Helm
Virginia City, Nevada

Can't you hurry this up a bit? I hear they eat dinner in Hades at twelve sharp. I don't aim to be late.

—Black Jack Ketchum
Clayton, New Mexico

Gentlemen, I am not used to this business, having never been hung before. Do I jump off or slide off?

—GEORGE SHEARS
Location unknown

CORONER'S VERDICTS

I declare this gent met his death at the hands of a doggoned good pistol shot.

—JUDGE ROY BEAN
Langtry, Texas
1893

The body was rich in lead but too badly punctured to hold whiskey.

—Provenance unknown
quoted by W. N. Burns, *Tombstone*

This man came to his death by suicide. He tried to shoot to death at the distance of a hundred and fifty yards a man armed with a Winchester rifle.

—quoted by MODY C. BOATWRIGHT
1946

There's always retribution for your deeds.

—CLINT EASTWOOD
Carmel, California
1973

First time I took this Outlaw Trail I was seven or eight. Helped push a bunch of cows through here, up the steep section from the Dirty Devil on over to Moab 'cross Dead Man Point and Horseshoe Canyon. Used to drive livestock all over here. Brought 'em down from Green River over from Hanksville and then south to New Mexico. In the old days people were tougher. Why, the people that lived over in Hanksville had to ride horses seventy-five miles to Green River to get the only doctor in the area. By the time you got there you was either dead or well. Undertaker did a hell of a lot of business.

—ARTHUR EKKER
Ekker Ranch, Utah
1975

I've labored long and hard for bread,
    For honor and for riches,
But on my *corns* too long you've tred
    You fine-haired sons of bitches.

—BLACK BART "THE PO 8"
southern California
c. 1880

That boy can handle a pistol faster than a frog can lick flies.
—ANONYMOUS COWPOKE
on seeing John Wesley Hardin
shoot five men who were firing at him
Abilene, Kansas
1871

As I was leaving Horse Creek one day a party of Indians "jumped me" in a sand ravine about a mile west of the station. They fired at me repeatedly, but missed their mark. I was mounted on a roan California horse—the fleetest steed I had, and laying flat on his back, I kept straight on for Sweetwater Bridge—eleven miles distant—instead of trying to turn back to Horse Creek. The Indians came on in hot pursuit, but my horse soon got away from them, and ran into the station two miles ahead of them. The stocktender had been killed there that morning, and all the stock had been driven off by Indians, and as I was therefore unable to change horses, I continued on to Ploutz's Station—twelve miles further—thus making twenty-four miles straight run with one horse.

—BUFFALO BILL CODY
on his Pony Express experiences
Independence Rock, Wyoming
1860

I ain't got no recollection of it.

—KIT CARSON
on seeing his picture on the cover
of a dime novel killing seven Indians
with one hand while holding
a greatly relieved maiden with the other
c. 1870

Bat's gun-hand was in working order, so I made him deputy. He patrolled Front Street with a walking-stick for several weeks and used his cane to crack the heads of several wild men hunting trouble; even as a cripple he was a first-class peace officer.

—WYATT EARP
on Bat Masterson
Dodge City, Kansas
1876

HOW TO IMPROVE YOUR FAST-DRAW

There is no use to hang a gun low unless it is held firmly to a position where the arm and hand can, by practice, learn to find it instantly. A sagging belt or any other arrangement that allows the gun pocket to swing or flap or twist will confuse the drawing.

—COTEAU GENE STEBBINGS
Texas panhandle
c. 1920

A pair of six-shooters beats a pair of sixes.

—BELLE STARR
Dodge City, Kansas
1877

Sitting by the table, I noticed that Wild Bill Hickok seemed sleepy and inattentive. So I kept a close watch on the other fellows. Presently I observed that one of his opponents was occasionally dropping a card in his hat, which he held in his lap, until a number of cards had been laid away for future use in the game. The pot had gone around several times and was steadily raised by some of the players, Bill staying right along, though he still seemed to be drowsy. The bets kept rising. At last the man with the hat full of cards picked a hand out of his reserves, put the hat on his head, and raised Bill two hundred dollars. Bill came back with a raise of two hundred, and as the other covered it he quietly shoved a pistol into his face and observed, "I'm calling the hand that's in your hat."

—BUFFALO BILL CODY
Deadwood, South Dakota
1876

Now, in regard to the position of Bill's body, when they unlocked the door for me to get to his body, he was lying on his side, with his knees drawn up just as he slid off his stool. We had no chairs in those days—and his fingers were still crimped from holding his poker hand. Charlie Rich, who sat beside him, said he never saw a muscle move. Bill's hand read aces and eights—two pair, and since that day aces and eights have been known as "the dead man's hand" in the Western country.

—DOC PIERCE, undertaker
Deadwood, South Dakota
1876

Judge Three-Legged Willie came into Shelby County and opened his court by tipping a flour barrel on its end and calling for the culprits. One local stepped forward and said the county didn't have no need of a judge and a court. The old judge demanded, "By what legal authority do you over-rule this court?" The fellow grinned and drove a bowie knife into the top of the flour barrel, saying, "This, sir, is the law of Shelby County." And before that knife could commence to quivering, the judge pulled out a long-barreled pistol and laid it on the barrel top. "If that's the law of Shelby County," he said, "then this here's the constitution."

—ANONYMOUS

VIGILANTES AROUND!!!
NO MORE MURDERS!!!
Behold the fate of this man. The same terrible end
awaits all murderers.
Life and the public security is too sacred not to be
protected, even by a resort to the unpleasant means
of *Lynch Law.*
TAKE WARNING! TAKE WARNING!
Else, ye murderers, the fate that this brute Schramie
has met with awaits you.

By Order of Committee
of *Vigilantes.*

—Notice tacked to a tree
from which a murderer had been hung
near Denver, Colorado

8
COWS

They shore ain't pretty and they don't smell good but there is somethin 'bout a cow that makes the man that owns one feel like he's got money in his purse.

—SPIN LUCETTE
Jenkins, California
1869

A slice of cow is worth 8 cents in the cow, 14 cents in the hands of packers, and $2.50 in a restaurant that specializes in atmosphere.

—JOE M. EVANS
El Paso, Texas
1939

Here's all you need to know about cows: They're not smart, they're bigger than you are, and some of them have absolutely no respect for human beings.

—TERRY HALL
Hastings, Nebraska
1993

Nearly all I know I have learned from a cow or in a cow camp. You'd be surprised just how much you can learn from a cow. The cow can teach you some very valuable lessons. Cows are regular in their habits, they go to the same place on the range to graze, they want to drink from the same place in a water trough, they are the best civil engineers you can find, and they can pick out the best possible grade to climb a mountain. A cow trail is always the best way to get out of a deep canyon. Follow a cow trail and you will come to water, or you will find the way out of a rough country if you are lost.

—DREW RUSH
Casper, Wyoming
1882

MAKING YOUR MARK

You put your brand on the hip and let him run, but of course there was much to it before you got that simple work done. First, you had to rope him. Sometimes, that took a whole team of men, for steers get bigger every day and you get older at the same rate. Some wild boy was always in a hurry to be the one that put the brand on, but one time around with a crazy steer gone mad from the hurt of it was usually enough. You had to stay on the boys, especially if they got the iron too hot—a small glow was enough, for more would make a messy mark and burn the hair off the steer.

—LEROY LENNOX
Oklahoma City, Oklahoma
1951

Grown cattle have a thick hide, but in branding calves, care must be exercised not to rock the corners of the iron, and burn through, but carefully burn a brand "cherry red," but not too deep. The burning faces of the branding irons were usually supposed to be oval, to avoid this burning through.

—CHARLES CAMP
Long Beach, California
1928

While it is easy to brand a calf, one has to keep a sharp lookout on its mother. As soon as she hears the cry of her young she will come at you like an express torrent.

—CAPTAIN GEORGE ASH
London, England
1923

COWS & MOTHERHOOD

The only practical knowledge I have gained in ranching is that a cow will have a calf.

—GEORGE LITTLEFIELD
Austin, Texas
c. 1875

If you teach a calf to lead, the old cow will follow.

—ANONYMOUS
Wichita, Kansas
c. 1880

Don't ever get between a calf and its mother—if she's a good mother, she's gonna charge you.

—FELIX ZUCKER
Pinole, California
1993

Never cower around a calving cow. Walk tall and know where you're going—and never, ever look down at your boots. You can clean them off later.

—Davy Buster
Burr Oak, Kansas
1955

We put a bell on an old cow for a leader, and when a yearling got lost from the herd, and came within hearing of that bell, it generally came back to the herd.

—John James Haynes
San Antonio, Texas
1920

CORRALING CATTLE

The uninitiated will probably be interested in knowing just how. Corrals, as we termed them, were built, when material was not so plentiful as now. The material was largely post oak rails, which we had cut and hauled by ox teams about five miles from the timbered country of Caldwell County. The posts were of fine cedar timber obtained from old Mountain City in Hays County. These corrals had to be much higher than the ordinary fence, as the infuriated Longhorns would, in their desperation to be free, try to go over the top or break them down. Once the material was on the ground, we dug deep, wide holes, about seven feet apart, and in these we placed two of the cedar posts in such juxtaposition as to hold the long rails which we piled one on top of the other until they reached the top of the high posts. That being done, some of the old-timers bound the ends of the posts together with wire or stout strips of rawhide, but at about the time of which I write we began to bind them with smooth wire. The sub-divisions spoken of above were divided into branding pens and horse corrals.

—G. W. MILLS
Lockhart, Texas
1922

COW MUSIC

Sounds like hogwash today, but a man who couldn't sing to calm a nervous cow wasn't enough cowboy to hold the job. At night, cattle get nervous, and anything could make them jump up and start, so you wanted a man with a voice good for keeping them quiet.

—JIMMY KENNEDY
Belfast, Texas
1916

The Texas Cowboy

WHAT TO SING TO A COW

I'm up in the mornin' before daylight
And before I sleep, the moon shines bright.
No chaps and no slicker, and it's pourin' down rain,
And I swear, by God, that I'll not night-herd again.
Oh, it's bacon and beans every day;
I'd rather be eatin' prairie hay.
I went to the boss to draw my roll;
He told me I was still nine dollars in the hole.
I'll sell my horse and I'll sell my saddle,
And you can go to hell with your Longhorn cattle.

> — "Old Chisholm Trail"
> Traditional
> c. 1870

Talkin' about music…. I used to own a saxophone, but traded it off for a cow. Made about the same noise and gave milk besides.

> —ANONYMOUS

HOW TO FIGURE A COW'S AGE

Range cattle with horns: In the cow's second year, the horns start a second growth and a small ring is seen encircling the horn. A second ring appears during the third year. These two grooves around the horn disappear as the animal becomes older. From three years on, the growth of the horns is marked by a groove that is much deeper. These rings provide an accurate basis for estimating the age of the animal. After the animal is three years old, the outer part of the horn plus the first ring are counted as representing three years, and each subsequent ring toward the base of the horn is counted as representing one year.

Polled (hornless) stock: A cow has temporary teeth for the first eighteen months or so. At two years of age, the cow will show two permanent center pinchers. At three years, two more permanent teeth form, and at four, two more. At five, the cow has reached maturity and all eight teeth on the lower jaw (cattle have teeth only on the lower jaw) will be large, permanent ones. After six years, the arch or curve of the teeth gradually loses its rounded contour and it becomes nearly straight by the twelfth year. In the meantime, the teeth have become triangular in shape and distinctly separated, showing a progressive wearing down to stubs.

—FAY WARD
Norfolk, Nebraska
1958

It is difficult to believe it, but in times of drouth [cows] actually eat cactus. But they do not eat the cactus because they like it. Every spine and tiny sticker, besides being barbed, is tipped with a poisonous venom as painful as the sting of a wasp. It makes a wound that swells and throbs and is slow to heal, but the cattle have to endure it. After breaking through the outer defenses of a tree-cactus, they eat it out from behind, then lie down with their noses stuck full of spiny joints and chew their cud complacently. The inside of their mouths becomes as tough as India rubber, and if they can get enough water to dilute the bitter juice they will live on cactus a long time.

—DANE COOLIDGE
Berkeley, California
1938

EXPRESS COWS

We had a stampede in the territory while Noah Ellis and myself were on herd together. In the run that followed my horse fell with me, and I thought the steers would run over me. But I soon learned that steers will not run over a man when he is down underfoot. They will run all around a fellow, but I have yet to hear of a man being run over by them.

—DICK WITHERS
Boyles, Montana
c. 1920

One of the slickest things I ever saw in my life was a cowboy stopping a cattle stampede. A herd of about six or eight hundred head got frightened at something and broke away pell-mell with their tails in the air and bulls at the head of the procession. But Mr. Cowboy didn't get excited at all when he saw the herd was going straight for a high bluff, where they would certainly tumble down into the cañon and be killed. You know that when a herd like that gets to going it can't stop, no matter whether the cattle rush to death or not. Those in the rear crowd those ahead, and away they go. But the cowboy spurred up his mustang, made a little detour, came in right in front of the herd, cut across their path at a right angle and then galloped leisurely on the edge of the bluff, halted, and looked around at that wild mass of beef coming right toward him. He was as cool as a cucumber, though I expected to see him killed, and was so excited I could not speak.

Well, sir, when the leaders had got within about a quarter of a mile of him I saw them try to slack up, though they could not do it very quickly. But the whole herd wanted to stop, and when the cows and steers in the rear got about where the cowboy had cut across their path I was surprised to see them stop and commence to nibble at the grass. Then the whole herd stopped, wheeled, straggled back, and went to fighting for a chance to eat where the rear guard was.

You see, that cowboy had opened a big bag of salt he had brought out from the ranch to give the cattle, galloped across the herd's course and emptied the bag. Every critter sniffed that line of salt, and, of course, that broke up the stampede. But I tell you it was a queer sight to see that man out there on the edge of the bluff quietly rolling a cigarette, when it seemed as if he'd be lying under two hundred tons of beef in about a minute and a half.

—S. L. LYMONS
Colorado Springs, Colorado
1898

SHIFTY FOREIGN COWS

Havoc on the hoof—that's a Brahma bull. A Texas-bred cross between the Brahma of India and the Mexican Longhorn, the Brahma is considered to be the most dangerous animal in rodeo. He's not content merely to buck, but usually seeks vengeance by attempting to gore his dismounted adversary. It takes real nerve to try to ride these huge, "ornery" beasts. There is only a rope around the bull for the cowboy to hold on to. A cowbell dangling from this rope under the animal's middle further infuriates him. As in bronc riding, one hand must be held free from the bull, and the cowboy must spur from shoulder to flank during the eight seconds which make a completed ride.

—MAX KEGLEY
Phoenix, Arizona
1942

Like any other animal, the Brahma bull is just as mean as man makes it. He is bold, and he is proud. [He is] the only type of steer that can look a man in the eye and not waver. The Hereford will look, then glance away. He remembers something that the two-legged creatures have done to him, and he

is ashamed of mankind. But the Brahma has no such scruples;
he neither fears nor disrespects the master of the beasts.

—ABEL P. BORDEN
Mackey, Texas
1934

TRANSPORTATION COWS

The last time I rode a bull I was a senior in college. When I
started playing with the Cowboys, they asked me to stop riding bulls, which was all right with me. I was looking for an
excuse to stop and still save face. "Oh, heck, I can't do this any-
more. Damn it. The Cowboys won't let me."

Thank God for the Cowboys.

—WALT GARRISON
Dallas, Texas
1988

COW SUBSTITUTES

I would rather not bore the public with buffalo.

—HORACE GREELEY
Reisinger's Creek, Colorado
1859

There were eleven buffalos in the herd and they were not more than a mile from us. The officers dashed ahead as if they had a sure thing on killing them all before I could come up with them; but I had noticed that the herd was making toward the creek for water, and as I knew buffalo nature, I was perfectly aware that it would be difficult to turn them from their direct course. Thereupon, I started toward the creek to head them off, while the officers came up in rear and gave chase. The buffalos came rushing past me not a hundred yards distant, with the officers about three hundred yards in the rear. I pulled the blind-bridle from my horse, who knew as well as I did that we were out for buffalos—as he was a trained hunter. The moment the bridle was off, he started at the top of his speed, running in ahead of the officers, and within a few jumps he brought me alongside the rear buffalo. Raising "Lucretia Borgia" to my shoulder I fired, and killed the animal at the first shot. My horse then carried me alongside the next one, not ten feet away, and I dropped him at the next fire. As soon as one buffalo would fall, [my horse] Brigham would take me so close to the next, that I could almost touch it with my gun. In this manner I killed eleven buffalo with twelve shots.

—BUFFALO BILL CODY
Cody, Wyoming
1879